Pressing
RESET
for the
Everyday
Person

Pressing RESET for the Everyday Person

Published by OS Press

ISBN 978-1-64184-074-3

Unless otherwise indicated, Bible quotations are taken from the New King James Version. Copyright © 1982 by Thomas Nelson, Inc. Used by permission. All rights reserved.

Original Strength

Your body is awesomely and wonderfully made. It was designed to be strong and capable throughout your life at every stage in your life. In fact, you are meant to be "anti-fragile," or not easily injured. You were made to endure life and all of its challenges.

Yes, life happens. Accidents happen. Injuries happen. But the human body is designed to heal and even prevent injuries IF it is moving and operating properly. This means you are never limited by your current physical and mental condition, at least you don't have to be. If you move the way you were designed to move, you can restore your strength, mobility, speed, and power. Mobility that was once lost can return. Pain that has nagged you for years can go away. Your body knows how to handle these limitations. You can even restore or gain your ability to focus, remember, interpret, and analyze information quickly; all through moving the way you were designed to move.

Moving the way you were designed does indeed make you anti-fragile. It restores your health and vitality. We call this your Original Strength. This is the strength you were created to have throughout your lifetime. This is the strength that allows you to perform your job and live your life better, the way you want to. It's the strength that gives you the freedom to move and the ability to enjoy your life. This strength lives inside of you, and it is released when you move according to your design. We call this Pressing RESET.

In this booklet, we are going to show you how to press the reset button on your body, how to move the way you were designed so you can restore the Original Strength you were meant to have.

Let's get started and learn how to Press RESET.

Pressing RESET

Your Original Strength is based on the Three Pillars of Human Movement. These are the pillars of movement we are designed to do each and every day. If we engage in these three things, we are Pressing RESET and strengthening the nervous system. These Three Pillars are:

1. Breathe deep with your diaphragm (belly breathe).

2. Activate your vestibular system (your balance and sensory integration system).

3. Engage in contra-lateral patterns (crawling, walking, marching) or mid-line crossing movements.

These three pillars are preprogrammed into each of our nervous systems. In fact, they are woven into the developmental sequence, the movements we moved through as children in order to become strong and anti-fragile. The purpose of the developmental sequence was to build your nervous system and strengthen your body so you could explore and conquer your world. These movements are still inside your nervous system today. If we engage in them again, they will do what they were designed to do: build your nervous system and strengthen your body. If we move like we did when we were children, if we remember how to breathe, move our heads, roll, rock and crawl, we can reestablish our Original Strength and essentially tie our bodies together so that we can happen to life, instead of life happening to us. In other words, we can Press RESET on our bodies and become strong, durable and able.

It might seem strange, but the developmental sequence can actually *develop* us at any age and any stage of our lives. The Five developmental movements we are going to remember how to do are:

1. Belly Breathe
2. Learn to control the movement of our eyes and head
3. Roll on the ground
4. Rocking back and forth
5. Crawling

These simple movements are the key to restoring our Original Strength.

Pressing
RESET

Belly Breathing

THE VERY BEGINNING OF STRENGTH

Why?

- You were born a "belly breather."

- Your diaphragm (main breathing muscle) is a spinal stabilizer and it helps to protect your spine. Proper diaphragmatic breathing allows you to move well.

- Breathing is the "bridge" between your autonomic nervous system.

  » Proper breathing calms your nervous system and keeps you in the parasympathetic mode (rest and digest mode).

  » Breathing up in the neck and chest excites your nervous system and keeps you in the sympathetic mode (fight or flight mode).

Position #1

BELLY BREATHING

- Lie in this position.

- Place your tongue on the roof of your mouth and close your lips.

- Breathe in and out of your nose and pull air deep down into your belly.

> It is super important that you learn to rest and keep your tongue on the roof of your mouth. This is where it belongs. It also helps your nervous system function optimally.

Position #2

CROCODILE BREATHING

- Lie in this position.

- Place your tongue on the roof of your mouth and close your lips.

- Breathe in and out of your nose and pull air deep down into your belly.

Don't make the mistake of dismissing how important breathing in your belly is. This is not just about getting air into your lungs. This is about building strength in your center. Your diaphragm is the chief stabilizing muscle in your inner core, it helps protect your spine.

Head Control

THE NEXT LAYER OF STRENGTH

Why?

- Controlling the movements of your head activates your vestibular system and improves its function.

  » The VS is your balance system and your sensory information collection point.

- Every muscle in your body is reflexively "wired" to the movements of your head.

- Head Control is essential to obtaining health and strength throughout your lifetime.

Movement #1

CHIN TUCK

- Lie in this position.

- Place your tongue on the roof of your mouth and close your lips.

- Raise and lower your head by tucking your chin to your throat and lifting your head off the ground as if to look through your knees.

- Lead the movement with your eyes.

- Do not hold your breath. Keep breathing through your nose.

Movement #2

QUADRUPED HEAD NOD

- Get into this position on your hands and knees.

- Place your tongue on the roof of your mouth and close your lips.

- Perform head nods by raising and lowering your head as far as your neck will allow you to move PAIN-FREE.

- Lead the movement with your eyes.

- Do not hold your breath. Keep breathing through your nose.

Movement #3

QUADRUPED HEAD ROTATIONS

- Get into this position on your hands and knees.

- Place your tongue on the roof of your mouth and close your lips.

- Rotate your head left and right as if you are trying to look at your "back pockets."

- Lead the movement with your eyes.

- Do not drop your head. Look over your shoulders.

- Do not hold your breath. Keep breathing through your nose.

RESET #3

Rolling

CONNECTING THE SHOULDERS TO THE HIPS

Why?

- Rolling further activates and strengthens the vestibular system.

- Rolling connects your shoulders to your hips, it connects your torso.

- Rolling nourishes the vertebrae of the spine.

- Rolling allows you to move fluidly and effortlessly.

Movement #1

THE EGG ROLL

- Lie on your back and grab your shins.

- Place your tongue on the roof of your mouth and close your lips.

- Leading with your eyes, look right, rotate your head to the right, then rotate your body to the right. Continue to look as far to the right as your body will allow.

- Then, look left, rotate your head to the left, then rotate your body to the left. Continue to look as far to the left as your body will allow.

Movement #2

THE WINDSHIELD WIPER

- Lie on your back and place your arms perpendicular to your torso.

- Bend your knees up toward your chest to lift your tailbone off the floor. Your feet will be in the air.

- Place your tongue on the roof of your mouth and close your lips.

- While keeping your shoulder blades in contact with the ground, rotate your legs from side to side.

- Keep your knees pulled up toward your chest even as you rotate your legs to the side. Do not let them drift away.

Movement #3

UPPER-BODY HALF ROLL – FROM BELLY TO BACK

- Lie on your belly with your arms overhead.

- Place your tongue on the roof of your mouth.

- Bend your right elbow, look at it, and reach for the floor behind you. Try to touch the floor with your elbow.

- Then roll back to your belly.

- Repeat this on the left side.

- Keep your lower-body relaxed throughout the movement.

Rocking

TOTAL BODY INTEGRATION

Why?

- Rocking further nourishes the vestibular system.

- Rocking integrates all the joints of the body into one whole body.

- Rocking coordinates the shoulders and the hips, preparing them for crawling and walking.

- Rocking soothes the nervous system as well as the emotions.

- Rocking restores posture.

Movement #1

ROCKING ON HANDS AND KNEES

- Get on your hands and knees.
- Put your tongue on the roof of your mouth.
- Hold your head up and keep your eyes on the horizon.
- Keep a tall sternum. Be "proud" and hold a big chest.
- Rock back and forth, shifting your weight over your hands and then back over your feet.
- Rock back as far as you can without losing your tall sternum.
- Keep your back flat. Do not let it round up or bow up.

> Feet can be in plantar flexion
> and/or dorsiflexion.

Movement #2

COMMANDO ROCKING

- Get on your forearms and knees.

- Put your tongue on the roof of your mouth.

- Hold your head up and keep your eyes on the horizon.

- Keep a tall sternum. Be "proud" and hold a big chest.

- Rock back and forth, shifting your weight over your forearms and then back over your feet.

- Rock back as far as you can without losing your tall sternum.

- Keep your back flat. Do not let it round up or bow up.

Crawling

TYING YOUR X TOGETHER

Why?

- Crawling connects both halves of the brain together, making it healthier and efficient.

- Crawling reflexively connects the body and ties it together.

  » It strengthens the nervous system.

  » It reflexively strengthens the body so that it can move efficiently, gracefully and powerfully.

- Crawling integrates other sensory systems with the vestibular system.

Movement #1

SPEED SKATERS

- Get on your hands and knees.
- Put your tongue on the roof of your mouth.
- Hold your head up and keep your eyes on the horizon.
- Keep a tall sternum. Be "proud" and hold a big chest.
- Move your opposite arm and leg back together.

Movement #2

HANDS AND KNEES CRAWLING

- Get on your hands and knees.

- Put your tongue on the roof of your mouth.

- Hold your head up and keep your eyes on the horizon.

- Keep a tall sternum. Be "proud" and hold a big chest.

- Move your opposite arms and legs together and crawl forward or backward.

Movement #3

LEOPARD CRAWLING

- Get on your hands and feet.

- Put your tongue on the roof of your mouth.

- Hold your head up and keep your eyes on the horizon.

- Keep a tall sternum. Be "proud" and hold a big chest.

- Keep your butt down, below your head.

- Move your opposite arms and legs together.

Movement #4

CROSS-CRAWLS

- Touch your opposite limbs together.
- You can touch hand to thigh, elbow to knees, etc.

Do not dismiss the simplicity of this movement. This movement can be the easiest and most effective entry point that begins the restoration and strengthening of the nervous system. This movement can help rewire the brain, overcome learning disorders and set the body free to move and express itself.

Your
DESIGN

The Power in Your Design

The power of movement restoration, the hope of healing, and the expression of strength all live inside your nervous system. Your very design contains the movement program intended to keep you strong, able and healthy.

Spending just a few minutes every day relearning or remembering how to do these movements will enable you to live your life better—with strength and health.

Your body truly is awesomely and wonderfully made. It is designed to be strong and able, always. Everything you need to experience this is inside your nervous system waiting for you to move with it. In other words, your Original Strength is inside. It's your move...

Simple Daily RESET Restoration Plan

FOR WHOLE BODY HEALTH AND STRENGTH

This is one of many simple daily restoration plans to help you restore your body, become resilient and live your life with health and strength. Again, this is simple, but please don't underestimate how effective this little plan can be. For best results, engage in the following routine daily, at least once:

Diaphragmatic breathing

While lying down in a comfortable position x three minutes—breathe in and out through your nose. Keep your tongue on the roof of your mouth. Focus on pulling air deep down into your belly. It may help to imagine trying to pull air down to your feet.

Why?

Because this is where strength starts. Breathing with your diaphragm makes you solid in your center, and it helps your body work at optimum hormone levels. It keeps you in "peace and harmony" mode and out of "fight, flight and panic mode."

Head nods

While lying on your belly, prop yourself up on your forearms. Lift your head up and down x 20 repetitions, moving as far as your head will let you move. DO NOT move into pain.

Simply move where your head will allow you to move. Oh, and lead with the eyes.

Why?

Because every muscle in your body is connected to the movements of your head. The body is designed to follow the head. Remembering how to move your head will, in a sense, sharpen and improve all the reflexive connections from your head to the rest of your body. This can help restore your reflexive strength!

Rolling around on the floor

Roll anyway you want to roll for three minutes: segmentally, egg rolls, backward rolls, frog rolls. Lead with your eyes and head when rolling. If you get dizzy, try slowing down or reducing the range of motion of your rolls, or try a different roll altogether.

Why?

Rolling sharpens your balance and feeds your brain with rich nourishment; it makes your brain healthy. Rolling also connects your center, layering more strength on top of the solid foundation that diaphragmatic breathing started. Rolling prepares your body to coordinate complex movements like running!

Rocking back and forth on all fours

Keep your head up, stay "proud" in your chest and rock your butt back towards your feet for three minutes. Rock back as far as you can go while maintaining a strong chest (flat back). DO NOT move into pain. You can move to the edge of it, just don't move into it.

Why?

Because rocking integrates all the major moving joints of your body. It makes you whole and prepares your body to move like a gently flowing stream, like poetry. You were made to move with grace. Rocking also sets and restores your posture.

Cross-Crawling

Touch your opposite limbs together alternating for three minutes. They should move fluidly, together. That is, your right arm should move along with and at the same time as your left leg. Breathe in and out through your nose and keep your mouth closed.

Why?

Because cross-crawling is the simplest engagement of your gait pattern (walking). It's also the movement that can tie your brain together and connect your whole body. It can make you whole in both brain and body.

Get Up

Practice moving from the ground to standing for three minutes. Lie down on the floor and stand up. Repeat. Do this in as many ways as you can think of. Be creative.

Why?

Though not necessarily a Big 5 Reset, your ability to get up off the ground easily will improve your longevity and your quality of life. We must always master our bodies' movements and resist gravity with ease. When gravity starts to win the battle, we lose our resiliency.

That's it. It's about 15 minutes of gentle movement that will allow you to live your life with strength: the ability to live and do the things you want to do in life. It is simple. It is not fancy or complicated, but it works.

The 3 Minute RESET

Don't have 15 minutes to spare today? Do you have three?

If you are pressed for time, have a hectic day, or you experience a particularly stressful situation, try the following three-minute reset. It will do your mind and body good.

1. **Breathe with your diaphragm x 1 minute.**
    Stop wherever you are—in whatever position you may be in—place your tongue on the roof of your mouth, and breathe deep down into your belly.

2. **Rock back and forth x 1 minute.**
    Find a place to do this; it is worth it. Get on your hands and knees, hold your head up and your chest "proud", keep your tongue on the roof of your mouth, continue to breathe down into your belly, and rock back and forth.

3. **Standing cross-crawls x 1 minute.**
    Touch your opposite limbs together, moving back and forth from side to side. Touch how you can—elbows to knees, forearms to thighs, or hands to hips.

Wherever you can reach comfortably, touch your opposite arm to your opposite leg repeatedly for one minute.
Do this and resume a less stressful or hectic and more energized day.

Want to learn more?

This booklet was designed to give a brief overview of the Original Strength System. We put it together because we know it can help everyone and anyone. If you do nothing more than what is in this booklet, you will notice many changes in how your mind and body begin to feel.

Original Strength is a human movement education company with a mission to transform the world by teaching people to move better, so they can live life better. We do this by conducting workshops, training and certifying coaches and instructors, developing educational materials for PE Teachers, Physical Therapy students, and professionals as well as many other professions dealing with fitness, health, and wellness, sports conditioning, vestibular and neuromuscular functionality.

If you want to know more about Pressing RESET and regaining your original strength, visit **www. originalstrength.net**. There you will find a variety of books, free video tutorials (Movement Snax), and a complete listing of our workshops and OS Certified Professionals near you.

You may want to consider finding an OS Certified Professional. These professionals will conduct an Original Strength Screen and Assessment (OSSA) which is the quickest and easiest way to identify areas your movement system needs to go from good to best. The OSSA allows a Pro to pinpoint the best place for you to start Pressing RESET and restoring your original strength.

Press RESET now and live life better because you were awesomely and wonderfully made to accomplish amazing things.

For more information:

óriginal
strength

Original Strength Systems, LLC
101 South Main Street, Suite 221
Fuquay-Varina, NC 27526

919.299.1774

www.originalstrength.net

"… I am fearfully and wonderfully made…"
Psalm 139:14

Made in the USA
Monee, IL
24 January 2022

89652545R00020